Helen Orme taught for many years before giving up teaching to write full-time. At the last count she had written over 70 books.

She writes both fiction and non-fiction, but at present is concentrating on fiction for older readers.

Helen also runs writing workshops for children and courses for teachers in both primary and secondary schools.

I Know Something

by

Helen Orme

RANS✺M

I Know Something
by Helen Orme
Illustrated by Chris Askham

Published by Ransom Publishing Ltd.
Radley House, 8 St. Cross Road, Winchester, Hampshire SO23 9HX, UK
www.ransom.co.uk

ISBN   978 184167 151 2
First published in 2013
Copyright © 2013 Ransom Publishing Ltd.

Illustrations copyright © 2013 Chris Askham

Siti Musa

Wall · Photos · Friends

Hi! I'm Siti Musa.

Siti is a Swahili (African) name meaning 'Lady'.

I'm the oldest in my family. I have two brothers, Daudi and Hanif, and a kid sister Afia.

My dad is a deputy head at our school, which can be bad news sometimes!

My mum is a social worker.

Lu Clarke

Wall · Photos · Friends

I'm Lu Clarke and I'm an only child. My dad is a businessman – he has an IT office in the town centre. My mum, who is Chinese, works in a bank.

My mum's parents (Po-po and Gong-gong – our name for grandparents) live by the sea. They used to have a Chinese restaurant and my mum worked there when she was younger. My other grandparents live close to us.

My parents want the best for me – but they don't always ask me what I want.

Kelly Jonson

Wall · Photos · Friends

I'm Kelly Jonson.

My mum is a single parent. She works as a solicitor. I've got an older brother, Jamie. His girlfriend is Susie.

My parents split when I was very young, and Dad remarried. We don't have any contact with Dad and his new family.

I really want to be a writer – oh, and I fancy Gary! I've decided that I want to be a vegetarian.

Rachel Phillips

Wall · Photos · Friends

I'm Rachel Phillips.

My parents split about 4 years ago. Dad runs a small printing business, and Mum is office manager at our school.

I live with Mum and spend weekends with Dad. His new wife is Janine. They have two young children, a boy and a new baby girl. It's O.K. visiting them, but I'd rather be with Mum.

My older brother Wil is at sixth-form college.

Donna Mills

Wall · Photos · Friends

I'm Donna Mills.

My dad's a bus driver and my mum works in a shop.

I have two older sisters, Marie and Briony. Marie's friend Susie is Kelly's brother's girlfriend.

My brother, Michael, is the youngest.

I love animals and going swimming.

There isn't much spare cash in our family – which makes things hard sometimes.

Chapter
1

Megan wasn't happy. Worse, Megan was really, really scared. It was time for school.

'Can't I stay home, Mum?' she begged. 'I don't feel well.'

'Don't be silly, you look fine,' said Mum. She gave Megan a friendly shove. 'Go on, I've got things to do.'

Megan picked up her bag. Maybe she wouldn't see him today. Maybe he wouldn't say anything to her.

Maybe it was going to be a good day.

* * * * *

She went into the form room. Ryan was there, but not Joe. She sat down. Sally would be here soon. Then she'd be O.K.

The bell went and everyone came in. Problem! Sally was away.

Megan felt bad again. She'd have to go to first lesson by herself. And he would be there.

She walked slowly out of the room. If she let him get there first, she could sit well away from him.

Chapter

2

It had started with a maths test. Joe was clever at maths. He also hated being beaten. The maths test was important and Joe wanted to come top. But Megan had beaten him, by a lot.

Joe couldn't take it. He wanted to make Megan feel as bad as he'd felt when Miss Harper read out the results.

Megan was shy. If someone was nasty to her, she just shut up. Worst of all, if it was really nasty she started to cry.

Megan had only been at the school for a few weeks. At first she had liked it. Most people were nice and Sally was really friendly. She was doing a great job looking after her.

But Joe wasn't going to look after anybody. After the test he got Megan alone in the classroom and said some really hurtful things. When she cried it made him feel good. It helped him feel big.

After that, whenever anything upset Joe he would look for Megan and have a go at her.

He told Megan what he'd do if she told anyone. He said everyone else knew she was a wimp. They wouldn't help her. She was on her own!

Chapter
3

Megan looked round the room. Where could she sit? There was a seat next to a gang of girls. She sat down in the spare seat. One of the girls turned and smiled.

'Hi,' she said. 'I'm Donna. You're Megan, aren't you?'

Megan nodded. She was pleased that the girl was being friendly.

'Do you know my sisters?' said Donna.

Megan looked at the others. What did she mean – 'sisters'?

Donna laughed.

'It's all right,' she said. 'We've just been friends for so long – that's what we call ourselves. That's Lu, Rachel, Kelly and Siti. Siti's the bossy one.' She laughed. The others laughed too.

Megan felt much happier. She really liked these girls.

At the end of the lesson Miss Harper hurried out. Donna and the others rushed off too.

Megan picked up her books. Joe didn't seem to be hurrying. As she went through the door he bumped into her. He pushed her hard against the door frame.

'Oh, sorry,' he said. 'I didn't see you there.'

He grinned nastily.

She turned round and faced him. This time she would say something.

'I've had enough,' she said. 'You've got to stop.'

Chapter
4

She'd been through it all in her head. In her head Joe looked at her, saw she meant it, said sorry and walked away. But real life was different!

'You stupid little … ' he started to say.

It wasn't working. Megan panicked. She lashed out and hit him on the nose.

Joe grabbed her arm and twisted hard. He was grinning.

Megan sobbed out loud. 'Let me go!'

'I'll let you go when I'm ready,' he said. 'D'you think you can hit me and get away with it?'

'I didn't mean it,' she gasped. 'I'm sorry.'

She was saying 'sorry' to him! It wasn't meant to be like that.

He grabbed her hair. He pulled hard. Her head felt as if it was burning. He was saying things now, horrible things.

She was bent over with pain. Why wasn't there anyone to help her?

'You're hurting me. Stop. Please.'

Chapter
5

Joe pushed her out of the way and went off laughing.

Megan was late for the next lesson, so she got told off. At break she went to the toilets, locked herself in and started to cry. She couldn't stand it any more.

'Who's in there? Are you all right?'

Megan didn't want to talk.

'Leave me alone. Go away.'

'Megan? It's me, Donna. What's wrong?'

She came out. All five of the girls were there. Siti took charge.

She put her arm round Megan.

'Tell us about it,' she said.

* * * * *

Next day the Sisters were waiting for Megan.

'Sorted,' said Siti. She showed Megan a small box.

'How's that going to help?' she asked, peering inside.

'Wait and see,' Siti laughed. 'I know something you don't know.'

* * * * *

The whole class was in the room when Siti got out the box. She went over to Joe.

'You think you're hard, don't you?' she said.

'Don't think, I know,' said Joe. 'Get out of my way.'

'You're just a nasty bully,' said Siti. 'You just pick on people who can't fight back.'

'Get lost!' Joe said with a sneer.

Everyone was looking at them.

Siti stepped back so everyone could see. Joe thought she was giving in. Then she tipped the box out onto Joe's desk.

Joe screamed, really loudly.

Siti picked up the mouse and pushed it towards Joe's face.

Joe was crying. He was nearly hysterical.

'Take it away. Get it off me.'

'It's a little baby mousy,' said Siti. 'And you're scared. Well, well, fancy that.'

Everyone was laughing. Who would have believed it? Joe – scared of mice.

Joe rushed out of the room.

Siti stroked the little animal. She looked at Megan.

'If he ever says anything to you again,' she said, 'You just say – tell it to the mouse!'

Siti's Sisters
The early years

– one year on:
the Sisters
are older

Helen Orme

Brother Bother
Illustrated by Cathy Brett

Helen Orme

Horsing Around
Illustrated by Cathy Brett

Helen Orme

New Man
Illustrated by Cathy Brett

Helen Orme

Who's Who
Illustrated by Cathy Brett

Helen Orme

Wet!
Illustrated by Cathy Brett

Helen Orme

Moving
Illustrated by Cathy Brett

– another year on:
The Sisters have grown up (well, nearly ...)

Helen Orme

Party Time
Illustrated by Chris Askham

Helen Orme

Shes My Friend Now
Illustrated by Chris Askham

Helen Orme

Leave Her Alone
Illustrated by Chris Askham

Helen Orme

Secret
Illustrated by Chris Askham

Helen Orme

Sleepover
Illustrated by Chris Askham

Helen Orme

Dont Do It!
Illustrated by Chris Askham